**Ask a question.
Start a conversation.
Strengthen a relationship.**

Here are more than 100 questions,
accompanied by rich and varied images
that are designed to stimulate conversation between parents and children.
The questions are provocative, the
images sometimes startling,
sometimes beautiful, and
always mesmerizing. This little book deserves a place on
every family's bookshelf.

My thanks to Donata Elschenbroich for the insights and ideas that I got from her book, *World Knowledge of Seven Year Olds*. They were the basis for the origin of this book. And I thank my family, especially my daughters Leonie and Silja, for their unfailing cooperation, patience, and love of fantasy.

Antje Damm

A Neal Porter Book
Published by Roaring Brook Press
A Division of The Millbrook Press, 2 Old New Milford Road, Brookfield, Connecticut 06804
First published in Germany by Moritz Verlag, Frankfurt on Main, in 2002

Library of Congress Cataloging-in-Publication Data on file

ISBN 0-7613-1845-3
1 2 3 4 5 6 7 8 9 10

Translated by Doris Orgel
Design by Michael Yuen
Printed in Belgium
First American edition 2003

Antje Damm

ask me

A Neal Porter Book
Roaring Brook Press
Brookfield, Connecticut

Who is your best friend?

Which of your dreams do you remember?

Have you ever seen animals in the sky?

What did you do in your mother's belly?

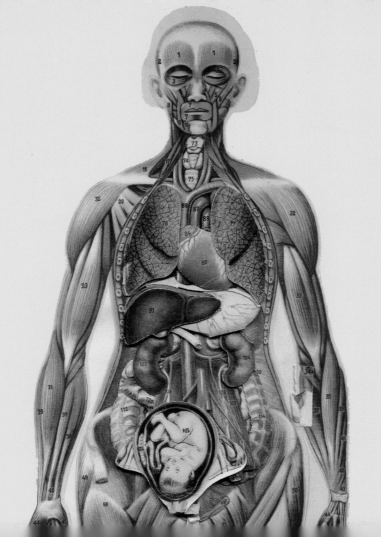

What do you like to smell?

What do you do when you're bored?

Where would you like to live someday?

What pet do you wish you could have?

What will you save for your own child?

Have you ever sent a valentine?
To whom?

Have you ever cooked something with your dad?

How can you tell that you're growing?

Is there something you don't like to eat?

What stories do they tell
about you as a baby?

Which of your pictures makes you proudest?

What kind of music do you like to make?

What was it like when you were born?

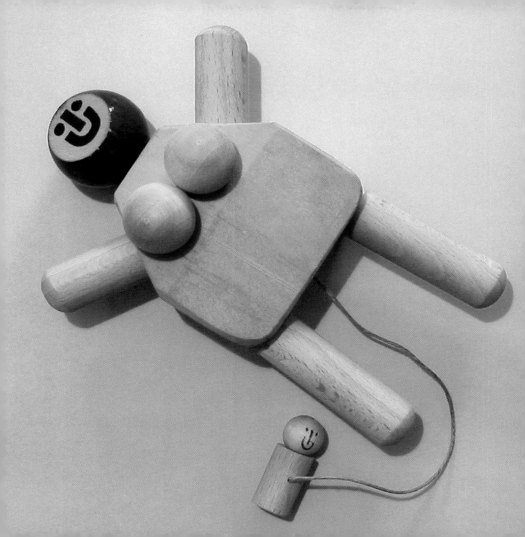

Is there a bad word that you think is funny?

What can your dad do really well?

Whom don't you like to kiss?

Have you ever picked fruit off a tree?

What book do you really like?

If you were king or queen, what would you change?

Do you know what your parents looked like when they were little?

With whom would you like to cuddle?

What do you like to collect?

Is there someone you can't stand?

AUNT IRMA

What can you do better than your parents?

How do you make people laugh?

What have your grandparents told you
about their childhood?

Which story can you tell?

Did you ever give an animal a name?

What special thing can you do with your hands?

What do you wish that could never come true?

What do you see when you
look out your window?

Were you ever all alone?

Did you ever write your name
in the sand?

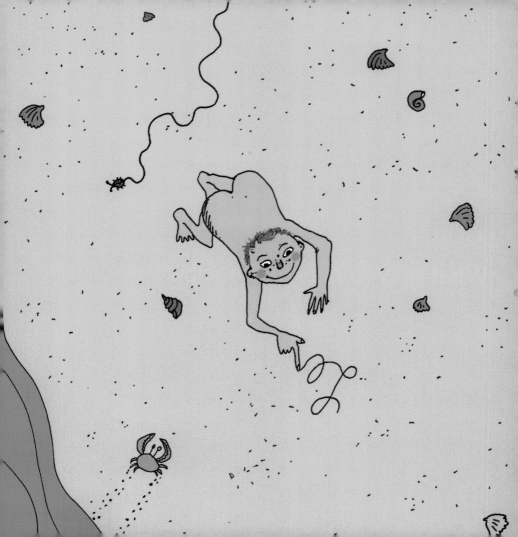

What do you play in the snow?

With whom would you like to trade places?

What makes you really mad?

Do you have a secret?

What do you do every day?

Do you want to have children someday?

What will you keep forever?

What do you wish you could do really well?

Who's in your family?

Did you ever make your own toys?

What color are your eyes?

What are you afraid of?

What kind of house would you like to
build for yourself?

Where would you like to travel?

Did you ever find a dead animal?
What did you do with it?

Do you have a guardian angel?

What do you do when nobody has time to play with you?

What's your favorite fairy tale?

What do you like to touch?

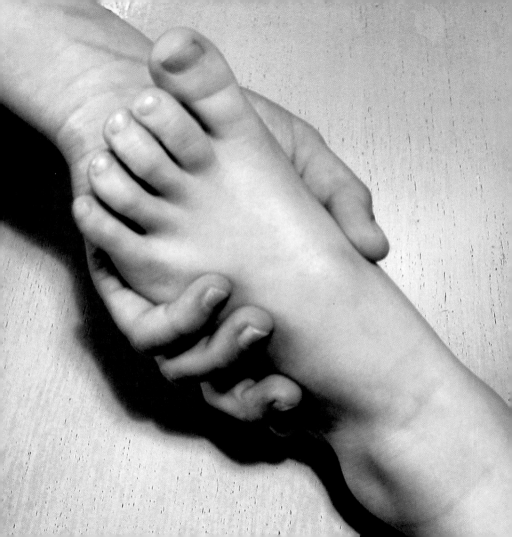

What noises do you hear in the morning?

Did you ever cut up a piece of fruit?
What did you find inside?

What rhyme can you make?

I have a cat.
His Name
is pat.

Did you ever play in the woods?

What have you brought back from a trip?

What do you do when you're freezing?

What do you like to do in the summer?

What's your favorite disguise?

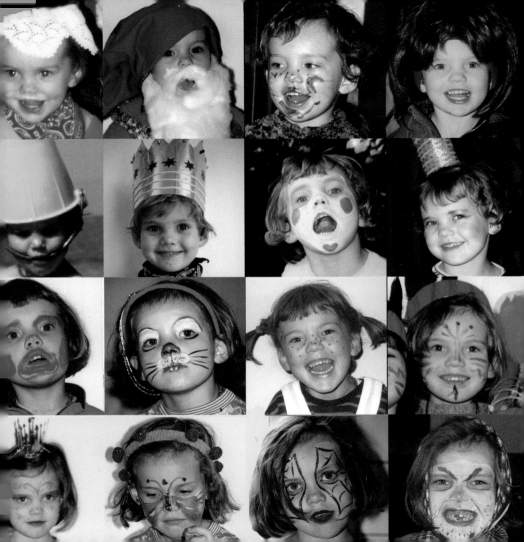

What makes you sad?

What do you like to paint?

Do you believe in gnomes?

How did your parents choose your name?

Have you ever been homesick?

What do you put on to look good?

Did you ever fix something that was broken?

Do you have any toys that your parents
played with when they were kids?

Whom can you talk to about everything?

Which animals scare you?

What's your favorite place to play?

What will you do when you're grown up?

Do you know what your grandparents played with when they were little?

Do you have little brothers and sisters?

What do you think is cute?

Did you ever watch an animal being born?

What was YOUR last fight about?

Did you ever comfort someone?

What would you like to know more about?

Do you sometimes help around the house?

172

What do you do that you shouldn't?

When do you eat up everything on your plate?

What animal would you like to be?

What makes you laugh?

What animal did you ever worry about?

Where do you like to hide?

What feels good on your skin?

Where in the world do you live?

What rules have you made?

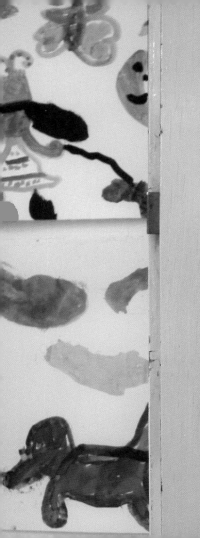

Did you ever see the moon rise?

Whom do you miss?

What have you taught someone?

What place do you know how to get to?

Is there anything good about being sick?

Where would you like to sleep tonight?

Where would you like to wake up tomorrow morning?

What are you investigating?

Whom did you nurse back to health?

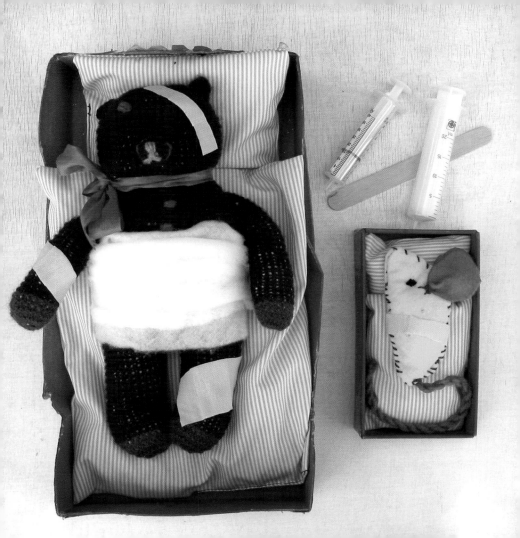

Where have you discovered footprints?

What do you like to build with?

What game have you invented?

Did you ever fall into a brook?

What do you need when you go to bed?

Did you ever paint a self-portrait?

Antje Damm was born in Wiesbaden, Germany, in 1965 and now works as an architect in Nuremberg. Since the birth of her daughters Leonie and Silja she has been interested in children's books and is now the author of several.